Recipes of the
Old German Restaurant

and other traditional
German Recipes

by Marzella Leib

Proctor Publications, LLC

Proctor Publications, LLC
P.O. Box 2498•Ann Arbor, Michigan 48106
800-343-3034
www.proctorpublications.com

PUBLISHER'S CATALOGING-IN-PUBLICATION DATA
(Provided by Quality Books, Inc.)

Leib, Marzella
        Recipes of the Old German Restaurant / Marzella
    Leib
        p. cm.
        Preassigned LCCN: 00-90848
        ISBN: 1-882792-96-3

        1. Cookery, German. 2. Old German Restaurant
    (Ann Arbor, Mich.) I. Title

        TX721.L45 2000   641.5943
                              QBI00-489

This book is dedicated to the many, many friends of the Old German Restaurant and the memories we'll always treasure.

Acknowledgments

I have been blessed with many loyal and supportive friends who have shared my desire to preserve the memory of The Old German Restaurant through the authentic German recipes of the food that was served there for over 70 years. Additional traditional German recipes have been added to this book, although they were not on the regular menu of the restaurant. Washtenaw County has always enjoyed a number of excellent German sausage makers, bakers and pastry chefs, and they supplied whatever was not created in our own kitchen.

Many people actively assisted in this project and I wish to acknowledge their encouragement and help.

- Robert (Bud) Metzger

- William (Bill) Dettling

- Reinhard Wittke

- Peggy Geiger

- Franz Leib

- Roland Steudle

- Grace Shakmann

History of the
OLD GERMAN RESTAURANT
Reinhard Wittke

From its founding in the early 1800s Ann Arbor was a very German town, attracting immigrants from southern Germany, primarily from Wuerttemberg. At one time Ann Arbor's population was almost 50% German. It continued to be a very German town into the post World War I era. A number of German restaurants, including the Old German, appeared on the Ann Arbor scene.

In 1928 William Schwarz, a trained butcher from Germany, and his wife Anny opened a modest German restaurant at 117 S. Ashley in what had once been a tire store with a gas pump. He named it the Old German. Beginning with only a counter and a few tables the restaurant flourished and soon took over the space of a grocery store around the corner on Washington Street. This unique " L" shape remained an Old German trademark throughout its existence.

The Old German was well located in busy downtown Ann Arbor. The

Germans of the second and third wards lived in the adjacent Old West Side area. Both German craftsmen and non-German workers from nearby factories, such as King Seely, American Broach, and International Radio (later Argus) would lunch at the Old German throughout the time of World War I and afterward.

The 1930s brought a number of changes to the Old German. Although the repeal of Prohibition in 1933 helped other restaurateurs, it did not help Bill Schwarz, because, as a non-citizen, he was denied a liquor license. Consequently, he sold the restaurant to the Haab family, who owned the Old German from 1934 to 1936, when it reverted to Schwarz. At that time Schwarz invited his friend, Gottlob Schumacher to become a partner. Schumacher's wife Caroline, a skilled cook, headed the kitchen. Under her direction the Old German turned out daily specials like chicken pot pie, pork hocks and sauerkraut. The influence of Caroline's home style cooking continued until the day the restaurant closed with her recipes for the famous vinegar and oil potato salad, cole slaw, and cucumber salad with onions. The Schwarz-Schumacher partnership continued until Bill Schwarz passed away. Schumacher then became the sole proprietor, and he and Caroline continued the Old German restaurant tradition until they sold it to Fritz and Bertha Metzger in 1946.

The Metzgers had immigrated to Ann Arbor from the southern state of Wuerttemberg, the Swabian area of Germany, in 1926. In 1929 they opened a German-American restaurant in Ypsilanti. When they moved to Ann Arbor in 1938, they opened the German Inn, which was located in the St. James Hotel on Huron Street, across from the bus station. In 1946 the Metzgers were looking for a new location and Gottlob Schumacher was looking for a buyer. The Old German was then sold to the Metzgers with the stipulation that they keep the Old German name. Although Gottlob sold the restaurant, it remained an important part of his life. He became a frequent patron and celebrated each birthday at the traditional round table. He was even present when the Old German finally closed its doors on March 15, 1995.

The Metzgers built on the foundation established by their Old German predecessors with their own style and flavor. The glowing success of the restaurant can be attributed to a number of factors. For one, the Old German was a family affair with Fritz Metzger out front and "Ma" Metzger supervising the kitchen. In 1946 when son Robert "Bud" returned from the armed forces after World War II, he began his Old German career. His sister Bert had already been active with the family business since the German Inn. Other members of the family also participated, especially Bud's son Mark, who became involved after the fire in 1975. Fritz Metzger's death in 1954 placed the Old German in the hands of Mrs. Metzger who oversaw the kitchen while Bud managed the operations. With the passing of Mrs. Metzger in 1972, Bud became the sole owner.

Robert "Bud" Metzger
1999

The Old German's kitchen supervised by Mrs. Metzger was outstanding. Bill Dettling, who had begun his Old German career in 1946 as a kitchen helper for Gottlob Schumacher, eventually became the chef under the tutelage of Fritz and "Ma". He took over the kitchen in 1972 and remained with the restaurant until it closed in 1995. A remarkable accomplishment, and possibly a chef's record for longevity.

The main attraction of the Old German, of course, was the food. Consistently excellent, it was authentically German and cooked from scratch on the premises. Visitors from Germany often commented on the authenticity of the food. Tourists who visited Germany often felt that the food at the Old German was even better than what they tasted abroad. The menu was varied and offered unusual items emphasizing primarily south German cooking. The famous Old German potato salad (still available locally), the Kaese Spaetzle (cheese spatzen), the stuffed noodle, faeddle soup (strips of very thin pancake in broth), Zwiebel Kuchen (onion pie), the liver dumplings and liver dumpling soup, along with the veal heart were unique. There were also the old standbys: beef rouladen, sauerbraten Old German style, the short ribs of beef, Hasenpfeffer, spare ribs and sauerkraut, Schnitzel, bratwurst, and many more. The Old German meat patties were a most popular item, a creation of Fritz Metzger. They were not a hamburger, but a meat patty. (See recipe on page 27)

"The proof may be in the pudding", but at the Old German the proof was in its distinctive German dishes. The Old German became a premier place to eat in Ann Arbor. A favorite gathering place for generations of University of Michigan students, faculty, alumnus, townspeople and visitors. It became a popular place to celebrate anniversaries, weddings, and after-game dinners. The old round table in its corner near the kitchen was a genuine Stammtisch, attracting a regular luncheon crowd that included lawyers, brokers, tradesmen, and local politicians. The counter remained a fixture to the end. Long lines waiting to gain admission attested to the popularity of the Old German.

Not to be overlooked was the ambience created by the congeniality of the family and staff. There was always someone, usually Bud or Bert, to warmly greet you at the door and invite you into the friendly confines of the Old German. Once inside you could not help but notice the relaxing classical background music, the magnificent collection of Mettlach steins, the beamed ceiling and the unique bar. Many old timers can recall the changes that took place over the years. When the Metzger family acquired the Old German in 1946, there was a metal ceiling, which was lowered in the early 1950s to hide the original. Later wall paper with Latin inscriptions was added. In 1962 the original bar was moved from the east wall to the west, and wooded beams and shelves appeared. As the collections of steins and artifacts increased, they were more prominently displayed. For a time paintings by local artists became part of the decor.

The devastating fire of April 1, 1975 completely gutted the Old German. After almost two very trying and difficult years the Old German reopened in March of 1977. The new Old German was designed by Hans Wiemer from Germany, a graduate of The University of Michigan School of Architecture and a friend of Bud's. The former Daisy Market to the east became an added room. The bar was relocated to the area of the original bar, occupying a position which could serve both the old and new rooms. Beautiful solid beams from northern Michigan graced the ceiling and walls. Replaced were the Mettlach steins and artifacts which had been lost in the fire. What emerged was a genuine old world atmosphere. However, one area remained unchanged— the counter and round table near the kitchen. Externally the facade was altered with the addition of an eye-appealing fifteen foot wrought iron sign depicting a beer wagon, hops and the fruit of the vine. This also became an Old German landmark.

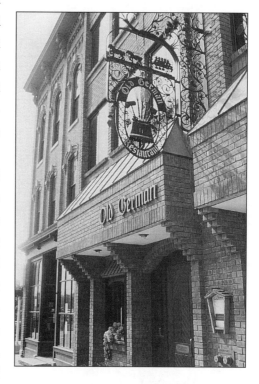

The aspects of the Old German, its caring family, good food, background music and old world setting, created more than just a restaurant. They created "Gemuetlichkeit", that special ambience enjoyed by an appreciative clientele.

The closing of the Old German on March 15, 1995 was bittersweet, made more so by the return of so many 'old timers' for one last visit. Many of them had their first beer, their first date, their after-game celebrations of victories or defeats, their engagements and wedding receptions at the "Old G". In an effort to keep some of the memories with us this Old German Cookbook was created. Thanks to Marzella Leib, an Old German wait person for many years, and Bill Dettling, its long-time chef, this cookbook preserves and makes available the recipes which brought so much enjoyment to so many.

Table of Contents

Breads 80

Appetizers

Herring Salad With Sour Cream
- *Heringstopf Mit Saurer Sahne*

Sour-cream sauce

1 cup sour cream

1/2 cup yogurt - unflavored

Juice of 1/2 lemon

1/4 tsp. sugar

     Blend all ingredients.

Salad

2 small onions

2 tart apples

8 marinated herring fillets

2 tsp. fresh dill or 1/2 tsp. dried dillweed

Peel onions and cut into thin slices. Peel and quarter apples, remove cores and cut into thin wedges. Blend onions and apples with sauce. In dish arrange herring and apple-onion mixture in layers. Cover tightly and marinate in refrigerator 5 hours.

     Sprinkle with dill and serve. Makes 4 to 6 servings.

Chef Bill Dettling in his kitchen at the Old German Restaurant.

Old German Zwiebel Kuchen

4 - 5 medium onions, sliced fine
6 OZ saltine crackers, crushed
1/2 tsp. salt
1/2 tsp. curry powder
2/3 stick margarine
2 cups milk, boiled
3 eggs
5 slices American cheese, sliced very fine

Boil sliced onions in water until tender and drain. Combine crushed saltines, salt, and curry powder. Melt margarine, add to dry ingredients, and mix thoroughly. Put 2/3 of this mixture on the bottom of 8" x 8" x 2" pan. Place drained onions on top of cracker mixture. Beat 3 eggs, add 2 cups boiled milk, pour over top of onions, and sprinkle with diced cheese. Top with remaining crackers. Bake in 425° oven about 20 minutes or until golden brown.

Tartar

1 1/2 lbs. fresh ground round
3 egg yolks
1 tsp. oil
1 tsp. tarragon vinegar
1 tsp. Worcestershire sauce

Mix ingredients together and serve on rye bread; top with hot mustard, salt, pepper and finely chopped onions. Garnish with parsley.

Soups

Oxtail Soup - *Ochsenschwanzsuppe*

2 - 3 tbs. fresh lard or butter

1 good size oxtail, cut into about 1" pieces at the joints

2 med. potatoes, diced and dried on paper toweling

2 small carrots, diced

1/2 leek, coarsely chopped

2 qts. water

1 small onion, finely diced

1 large bay leaf

4 tbs. flour

Pinch of thyme

Pinch of paprika

5 or 6 peppercorns

Madeira or sherry wine

3 tbs. butter

Salt

Heat lard or butter in 3-quart saucepan, add diced vegetables and oxtail pieces and brown slowly. Pour cold water into meat and vegetables, add bay leaf, thyme and peppercorns. Bring to a boil, reduce heat and simmer covered for 2 hours. Remove oxtail pieces, trim meat from bones and dice. Return diced meat to soup and discard bones. Heat 3 tbs. butter in small skillet, add diced onion and cook until golden brown, but not blackened. Stir in flour, blend with butter and let brown slowly to cocoa color. Ladle a cup or so of hot soup stock into this mixture gradually, stirring to keep it smooth. Pour this mixture back into soup, stirring as you do so. Let soup simmer another 30 minutes. Season with paprika, wine and salt to taste.

Liver Spatzen Soup - *LeberSpatzen Suppe*

1 oz. beef liver
1/2 lbs. ground pork
1 egg
1/4 rib celery
1 green onion
Pinch of nutmeg
Pinch of salt
Flour

Put all ingredients, except flour, in food chopper and chop fine. Add flour to make a thick paste, like spatzen dough. Boil beef stock and press mixture with spatzen press into boiling beef stock. Cover and let simmer for 2 minutes. Sprinkle chopped parsley on top and serve.

Vegetable Soup - *Geinuese Suppe*

About 8 oz. prepared vegetables (cauliflower, shelled green peas, carrots, kohlrabi, brussel sprouts, asparagus, cabbage)
1 1/2 oz. butter or margarine
3/4 oz. flour
2 1/4 pints stock (4 1/2 cups)
Salt and meat extract or other seasoning to taste

Trim, wash, and chop or slice the vegetables. Leave peas whole and separate cauliflower into flowerets. Fry for a few minutes in the hot fat, sprinkle in the flour and cook a little longer. Gradually pour in the hot stock, bring to a boil. Turn down the heat and simmer gently about 40 minutes until all the vegetables are cooked. Season with salt and meat extract to taste.

Liver Dumpling - *Leberknoedel Suppe*

2 oz. ground liver

1 lb. pork, ground extra fine

3 eggs

1 tsp. salt

1/4 tsp. pepper

Ground nutmeg to taste

2 or 3 sprigs of parsley, chopped

1/4 cup flour or enough to bind

2 beef bouillon cubes

Mix all ingredients together. Form into balls (if you keep your hands slightly wet, dumplings will not stick). Bring 2 quarts of water to a boil. Add bouillon cubes and 1/2 tsp. salt. Drop dumplings into boiling water. Bring back to a boil and simmer without covering 20 - 30 minutes. After removing dumplings from liquid, skim any grease off the top of stock. This will remove bitter flavor. Add a little more hot water to the stock if is bitter. Note: Have water boiling as you form your dumplings, and drop them into the water as you make them or the dumplings will not hold together.

Old German *Goulash* Soup

1/4 cup margarine

1 lb. pork, 1/2" dice

4 med. onions 1/2" dice

2 large green peppers, 1/4 - 1/2" dice

1 can diced tomatoes (14 1/2 oz.)

2 beef bouillon cubes

1/2 tsp. salt

1/2 tsp. pepper

2 Tbs. paprika

1/4 tsp. garlic powder

1 tsp. lemon juice

1 tsp. caraway seed

1 tsp. Maggi

6 drops Tabasco sauce

4 med. potatoes, cooked and diced

1 qt. beef stock or water

Brown meat with margarine until medium brown. Add 1 quart beef stock, diced pepper and tomatoes. Cook 1 hr. 15 min. or until meat is tender. Add 4 med. cooked, diced potatoes and bring to a boil. Melt 1/4 stick margarine, add 1/4 cup flour to make a brown roux. Add to soup and return to boil, which will thicken soup. Remove from heat as soon as it is thick.

Swabian "Flädle" Soup

6 1/2 oz. flour
2 eggs
Pinch of salt
1/2 cup milk
Small amount of frying fat or oil
6 cups meat broth

Mix the flour, eggs and salt until smooth and let stand for about 1/2 hour. In a pan, bake flat, round pancakes (Flädle), tilting the pan when filling in the dough to coat the bottom of the pan thinly. Cut into strips and serve in hot meat broth.

Brätstrudel Suppe

6 1/2 oz. "Kalbsbrät" (ground veal)
4 tbs. heavy cream
1 tbs. parsley, chopped
1/2 lemon
1/4 tsp. thyme
Pinch of nutmeg, ground
6 cups meat broth

Prepare Swabian Flädle as described above. In a bowl, mix well the Kalbsbrät, heavy cream, parsley, grated lemon rind, thyme and nutmeg. Spread in a 1" layer on the Flädle, roll up and let stand for 15 minutes. Cut into 1 1/2" bits and place carefully into the simmering broth and let them draw for 5 minutes.

Chicken Broth
- Huehnerkraftbruehe oder Huehnersuppe

1 5-6 lb. chicken
1 veal knuckle (optional)
3 qts. water
Vegetables - 1 carrot, 1 small onion, 1 rib celery
Salt to taste

Wash and singe chicken. It may be cooked whole, or quartered, depending on what you intend to do with it afterwards. Put chicken or washed veal knuckle in cold water and add vegetables. Use a tall soup pot so that water will cover chicken. Bring water to a boil, cover pot and let soup simmer slowly one hour, skimming foam from surface as it rises. Add salt and simmer slowly another hour. Check seasoning and add more salt if necessary. Remove chicken and bone, then strain soup through a fine sieve. Cool and skim fat from surface. Store in refrigerator, or heat and serve. Chicken may be sliced or diced and served in soup along with vegetables or fine noodles. Sprinkle with finely chopped parsley or chive before serving. Chicken may also be used for salads, fricassee or chicken pot pie. If you want a very clear, light soup, do not use veal knuckle or other bones.

Pea Soup - *Erbsen Suppe*

1 lb. dried peas
2 slices bacon
2 stalks celery
1 med. onion
1/2 qt. beef stock
Salt to taste
Maggi, to taste
Nutmeg, to taste

Cook peas, diced celery and onion in beef stock. Add fried diced bacon. Cook 1/2 hour, or until well done. Add Maggi, salt and nutmeg to taste.

Lentil Soup - *Linsen Suppe*

1 lb. lentils
1 bay leaf
1/3 cup vinegar
1 carrot
1 1/2 stalk celery
2 bouillon cubes or beef stock
1 med. onion
Brown flour

Cover lentils with water, and bring to a rolling boil. Drain water and add fresh water along with bay leaf, vinegar, bouillon cubes or stock and cook until done. Thicken with browned flour. Dice all vegetables and cook separately in boiling water until done. Drain vegetables and add to thickened soup. Season to taste with Maggi, salt and pepper.

11

Tomato Soup - *Tomaten Suppe*

1 can 46 oz. tomato juice
1 can 14 1/2 oz. diced tomatoes
1/2 small onion, diced fine
Garlic to taste
2 Tbs. cornstarch
1 1/2 cups milk
Nutmeg, to taste
Maggi to taste

Bring tomato juice and diced tomatoes to a boil. Add cornstarch mixed with a little water to thicken soup. Add milk and bring to a rolling boil, stir often, remove from heat. Add nutmeg and Maggi, then serve.

Mushroom Soup - *Pilz Suppe*

1 pint beef stock
1/2 stalk celery, chopped fine
1/3 onion, chopped fine
13 oz. can mushroom stems and pieces
10 oz. can cream of mushroom soup
Maggi

Sauté onion and celery in a little beef stock. Add remaining beef stock, mushroom pieces, and mushroom soup. Bring to a boil and simmer for a few minutes. Add Maggi to taste.

Potato Soup - *Kartoffel Suppe*

4 med. potatoes, peeled and diced

2 potatoes grated, to be used to thicken soup

2 stalks celery, same dice as potatoes

1 large onion, same dice as potatoes

Beef stock or beef bouillon

1/2 bay leaf

Diced leek to taste

2 slices bacon, diced

Nutmeg, Maggi, and salt to taste

Fry bacon until done. Cook potatoes, onion, celery and leek in 1 qt. stock, until just tender. When potatoes are tender and the soup is almost done, add bacon, the two grated potatoes, nutmeg and Maggi to taste. (Potatoes must be grated just before they are added to the soup. If they are allowed to sit, they will turn black.)

Onion Soup - *Swiebel Suppe*

1 large Spanish onion

7 1/2 cups beef stock or buillion

1/2 clove fresh garlic or garlic powder to taste

Chef seasoning or Maggi to taste

Pinch of salt

Melt a little lard in stock pot. Simmer sliced onion 20-30 minutes till light brown, stirring often. Add soup stock or bouillon along with spices and simmer 1/2 hour.

Add cheese of your choice for topping.

Note: If you cook onions until dark brown or black the soup will be bitter.

Entreés

Rouladen

10 thin slices beef (8" long x 4" wide x 1/4" thick)
1 quart beef stock or use 2 bouillon cubes with 1 qt. water
1 bay leaf
1/4 tsp. garlic powder
1 Tbs. paprika
Salt and pepper to taste
Juice from 1/2 lemon
1 small onion chopped fine
3 celery ribs chopped fine
10 slices bacon

Blend together celery, onion, and lemon juice. Spread strips of beef on table, top with one strip of bacon, then a small amount of celery mixture; salt and pepper to taste. Roll the beef strips lightly together, as you would a jelly roll, securing with a toothpick.

Fry beef rolls in a small amount of oleo or margarine until brown, reserving drippings for gravy. After beef is brown on both sides, place in roasting pan.

Brown gravy: Combine beef drippings with flour; allowing this to brown will make a brown gravy. Add the beef stock; bay leaf, garlic powder, and paprika. Bring to a boil and allow to thicken to a medium gravy. You may use Kitchen Bouquet for a browner gravy. Pour gravy over Rouladen and bake covered at 425° for about one hour or until meat is tender.

Salisbury Steak

1/2 lb. ground pork
1/2 lb. ground beef
1 rib celery, chopped fine
1 small onion chopped fine
1/4 tsp. salt
Garlic powder, salt and pepper to taste

Form this mixture into patties and fry in skillet until done.

Mushroom Gravy:

2 cups mushrooms
1/3 stick margarine
2 onions, thinly sliced
1/3 cup flour

Melt butter, sauté onions until tender then add flour and 2 cups of beef stock or water. Bring to a boil and add mushrooms with juice. Cook, stirring until thickened then pour over meat and serve with noodles.

Short Ribs of Beef

1 lb. short ribs (bone in) per person
1 medium onion
1 stalk celery
1 carrot
Salt & pepper

Place short ribs and other ingredients in large pot. Bring to boil and simmer for 1 hour 20 minutes. Trim fat, remove bone, and cut into chunks. Place in a small roasting pan, lightly salt and pepper and add a small amount of chopped onion on top. Put under the broiler for 5 minutes until top is nice and brown. Cut the cooked carrot and spread over top. Add short rib stock or steak sauce.

Ground Beef - *Hackfleisch*

1 lb. course ground beef
2 celery ribs, chopped
1 1/2 medium onion, chopped
Beef stock or water with bouillon
1 14 1/2 oz. can diced tomatoes
1 1/2 Tbs. cornstarch
Salt, pepper, garlic, Maggi to taste

Lightly brown meat in 425° oven. Cover with celery and onion and leave in oven another 15 minutes to sauté meat, celery and onion together. Add stock to cover 1" above meat. Cook for 15 minutes and thicken with cornstarch. Add tomatoes, salt, pepper, garlic and Maggi and a little Kitchen Bouquet. Serve over noodles.

Entree items at The Old German Restaurant included several different kinds of sausage — *Old German Bratwurst, Knackwurst* and *Blutwurst.* However, these sausages were not created at the restaurant.

Bratwurst was simmered in water for a few minutes and then fried with onion rings until golden brown. Bratwurst was served with potato salad or sauerkraut.

Knackwurst was also simmered until hot and served with potato salad, sauerkraut, and mustard.

Blutwurst was also simmered until hot and served as the other two sausages. However, blutwurst would run if allowed to boil and get too hot.

Roasted Chicken - *Huhn Gebraten*

1 chicken or two very small chickens, cleaned
1/4 cup Canola oil
1 tsp. salt
2 tsp. paprika
6 medium potatoes, pealed and diced 1 inch
4 slices bacon, cut into 1 inch strips
4 to 6 small onions, diced
1/4 cup hot beef bouillon
Parsley sprigs for garnish

Heat oil in large Dutch oven. Add chickens and brown well on all sides for 10 minutes. Season with salt, pepper and paprika. Continue cooking for another 10 minutes, turning often. Add potatoes and bacon and cook 5 minutes. Add onions and hot beef broth. Cover and bake at 350° for 45 minutes. Remove cover and bake 5 minutes more. Serve

Fried Chicken

2 lb. chicken, cut up
1 medium onion
1 stalk celery
Salt & pepper

Boil chicken in water with onion and celery until done, but not falling off the bone. Cool, sprinkle with salt and pepper, roll in flour. Place just enough Canola oil in frying pan to keep chicken from sticking, and place skin side down. Fry until brown. Serve with chicken gravy and dressing. Serves three people.

Chicken Giblets

1 1/2 lbs. chicken giblets and hearts
1 rib celery, diced
1 small onion, diced
1 carrot, sliced
1/4 stick margarine
1 1/2 tbs. flour
12 oz. boiling chicken stock (you may substitute 12 oz. water
     with 2 chicken bouillon cubes or chicken stock)
1 small bay leaf
Wine to taste

Boil giblets and hearts in water until tender, drain well, and slice into small pieces. In separate pan, cook celery and onion which has been cut into 1"- 1 1/2" pieces and cook in water with carrot until tender, and drain. Melt margarine, stir in flour to make a roux, add chicken stock, bay leaf, and wine. Add giblets and vegetables to gravy. Egg shade coloring may be used for additional color.

Chicken Liver - *Huehner Leber*

1 lb. chicken livers, cut up
1 Spanish onion, sliced fine
1 oz. Southern wine
Maggi

Saute onions and set aside. Fry liver in 2 tbs. of oil for 3 - 4 minutes. Put onion on top of liver, add a couple of drops of Maggi and cook until tender. Sprinkle with wine. Serve over toast. Serves two.

Bauern Omelette - *Eierpfannkuchen*

3 eggs

Very small amount of water

Polish sausage or salami, cut up

Swiss cheese, diced

Swiss cheese, strips

Salt & pepper

Beat eggs and water, add salt & pepper and cook in omelette pan. Sprinkle sausage or salami and diced cheese on top. Fold omelette together. Put Swiss cheese strips on top of folded omelette and put under broiler until cheese is melted.

"Brownie" Brown and Bud Metzger in the 1950s

Creamed Chicken

8 chicken breasts, split and boneless
1 bay leaf

Cook chicken and bay leaf in water about one hour or until
tender. Drain. Cut into pieces.

White sauce:

1/4 cup margarine or butter
1/4 cup flour
1/2 tsp. salt
1/4 tsp. pepper
Chicken stock base or chicken bouillon cubes
         or 1 cup milk for cream sauce
1/4 cup white wine
1 tbs. diced red pepper or pimento
Egg shade coloring

Heat margarine in sauce pan over low heat, stirring constantly,
add flour to make a paste, and stir until smooth and bubbly. Remove
from heat; stir in milk or stock and wine. Return to a boil and boil for
one minute, stirring constantly.

Add cut chicken pieces along with chopped pepper or pimento.
Add chicken bouillon to taste with a few drops of egg-shade coloring.

Serve over spatzen or biscuits.

Hasenpfeffer

Cut up two rabbits

Marinade:
2 tbs. sugar
1 bay leaf
1 tsp. salt
1/2 tsp. pepper
1/4 cup chili sauce
1/2 cup apple cider vinegar
1/2 tsp. garlic powder or 1/2 clove fresh garlic
1 med. onion, cut in half

Cover rabbit with marinade. If necessary, add enough water to cover 1" over rabbit. Marinate rabbit for two days.

Gravy:

Drain liquid from marinade into sauce pan. Add one 10 oz. can Campbell's Tomato Soup; bring to a boil. Thicken the sauce with brown flour. Put rabbit in a roasting pan; cover with gravy and bake covered at 425° about one hour or until done.

Fresh Pork Loin

3-4 lbs. pork loin
1 lb. can sauerkraut

Place pork loin and sauerkraut in roasting pot—add water to cover. Bake at 425° for 2 to 3 hours or until done. If a smoked loin is used, rinse sauerkraut well to remove salt.

Smoked Pork Loin - *Kassler Rippchen*

Place a 4 lb. loin into a large stock pot. Cover with cold water. Bring to a boil and simmer. Loin is done when you can put your finger into the loin easily. Good for shank or pork hock.

If desired, you could boil smoked pork loin in sauerkraut 1 1/2 hours or until done.

Testing the gravy.

24

Schnitzel

5 - 6 slices pork about 1/4" thick
> (pork, veal cutlet or fresh ham)

Salt & pepper

Flour

3 eggs

1/2 cup milk

Bread crumbs

Lemon Juice

Salt and pepper each slice and add a little lemon juice. Roll in flour so they are well coated.

In a separate bowl beat eggs, add milk, and mix well. Dip flour coated meat into egg wash, then into bread crumbs. Let stand for 1/2 hour at room temperature, and fry in hot oil until golden brown.

Spare Ribs - *Rippespeer*

1 slab pork ribs

1 1/2 sliced onions

1 bay leaf, crumbled

Cut ribs into strips with 2 ribs per piece. Put into roasting pan meat side up. Add onions, bay leaf and salt and pepper to taste.

Put uncovered in a 425° oven and let brown. Add 1" of water to pan, cover and let steam about 45 minutes or until done.

Stuffed Pork Chop - *Gefüellte Kottlet*

8 center cut pork chops

3/4 lb. ground pork

15 - 20 slices of bread or rolls

1/2 cup chopped onion

1/2 cup chopped celery

1/4 tsp. dry parsley

Salt and pepper to taste

2 cups chicken or beef stock or bouillon cubes

3 eggs

Nutmeg to taste

Dressing:

Sauté celery and onion with a small amount of stock. Add and mix remaining ingredients. Add only enough of the remaining stock to make a moist, but not wet dressing.

Salt and pepper one side of each pork chop, and fill with dressing (dressing may be placed on top of chops, if desired) and place in a roasting pan. Add about 1/2" of stock, sprinkle top of dressing with paprika. Cover roaster and bake at 425° about 1 hour. Dressing should be evenly browned on top.

Ochsenmaul Beef Tongue

1 beef tongue

1 cup cider vinegar

2 large onions

1 tbs. pickling spices

1 tsp. curing salt (Kosher)

1 tsp. sugar

1/2 cup water

1/3 cup cider vinegar

Garlic powder to taste

Cover tongue with water and boil with curing (Kosher) salt and cider vinegar until done. Rinse in cold water. Peal skin off tongue and divide in half. Slice one half of tongue into small slices and place in a quart jar,—layering with sliced onions. Mix 1/3 cup cider vinegar with 1/2 cup water, garlic powder, sugar and pickling spices. Pour over sliced tongue and onions to fill jar. Seal and refrigerate. Let stand for several hours before serving. If vinegar taste is too strong, drain and add water.

Meat Patties - *Frikadellen*

1 lb. ground pork

1 1/2 lbs. ground beef

1/2 lb. cooked pork or ground beef

1/2 tsp. onion

1/2 tsp. salt / 1/3 tsp. pepper

1/2 tsp. dry parsley or fresh parsley, chopped

3 slices dry bread or rolls

Run bread and meat through food chopper. Mix all ingredients together. Form into patties and fry.

Stuffed Noodle - *Maultaschen*

Dough:

2 cups flour

Salt and pepper to taste

3 eggs (reserve one egg)

1/4 stick soft margarine

Mix all ingredients together. If dough is too soft, add a little more flour. If dough is too hard add one more egg. Flour your work surface and roll dough out like pie dough. Beat remaining egg and spread over noodle dough.

Filling:

1 to 1 1/2 lbs. ground pork

1/4 cup onion

1/4 cup celery

1/2 tsp. dry or fresh parsley, chopped

Salt, pepper and nutmeg to taste

2 large eggs

Run pork, onion and celery through a food processor or chop very fine. Mix all ingredients well to a smooth paste and spread on top of noodle dough. Roll noodle dough and spread together like a jelly roll. Cut rolled dough into 2" circles and drop into boiling stock to cook for 20 minutes. After noodle circles are done, remove from stock to serve with gravy or with stock as a soup.

Stuffed Cabbage - *Kohlrouladen*

1 large head of cabbage cooked until leaves separate

1 cup cooked rice

1 1/2 medium onions, chopped fine

3 ribs celery, chopped fine

14 oz. can diced tomatoes

1 1/2 lbs. ground beef

1/2 lb. ground pork (use up to 1/2 lb. cooked meat leftovers)

1/3 tsp. black pepper

1/2 tsp. salt

1/3 tsp. garlic powder

1/2 tsp. paprika

8 oz. sauerkraut

1/2 tsp. caraway seeds

1/2 tsp. fresh chopped or dry parsley

Mix together all ingredients except cabbage. Peel cabbage leaves and roll 5 oz. of mixture into each leaf. Place in baking dish and cover with a can of tomato sauce. Bake covered for 1 hour 15 minutes.

Corned Beef and Cabbage

Place corned beef in 5-quart Dutch Oven. Add enough cold water just to cover. Add onion and garlic to taste. Heat to boiling and reduce heat. Cover and simmer for about 2 hours, or until corned beef is tender.

Remove corned beef to warm platter; keep warm. Skim fat from broth. Add cabbage. Heat to boiling; reduce heat. Simmer uncovered 15 minutes. Serves 6 to 8.

Boiled Dinner

Decrease simmering time of corned beef to 1 hour 40 minutes. Skim fat from broth. Add 6 small onions, 6 medium carrots, 3 potatoes, cut into halves, and, if desired, 3 turnips, cut into cubes. Cover and simmer 20 minutes. Remove beef to warm platter; keep warm. Add cabbage. Heat to boiling; reduce heat. Simmer uncovered until vegetables are tender, about 15 minutes.

Koenigsberger Klopse

1 lb. ground pork
1/3 lb. ground veal
1/2 small onion, chopped
2 ribs celery, chopped
Juice of 1 lemon
2 oz. finely chopped anchovies, sardines or herring,
        including oil
1 oz. green capers
2 tbs. flour
1 tsp. salt
1/4 tsp. pepper
1 tsp. chopped parsley, fresh or dry (fresh gives better flavor)
3 large eggs, beaten

Add chopped onion, celery, lemon and anchovies together in food processor. Add to pork and veal. Stir in 2 tbs. flour. Season with salt, pepper and parsley; mix in eggs. If dough is too thin, add a little more flour.

Stock:
2 qts. water
Put rest of lemon with peel into the water
1 med. onion cut in half
1/2 cup cider vinegar
1/3 tsp. pickling spice
1/4 cup dry white wine

(Continued on following page)

Koenigsberger Klopse continued

Salt and pepper to taste

Bring stock to a boil. Form meat into balls about 3 oz. size. Drop meatballs into stock and simmer 20 minutes. Remove *klopse* from stock and place in serving dish. Remove onion and lemon and discard. Add capers to stock for use in gravy.

Gravy:

1/4 cup butter or margarine, melted

1/4 cup flour to make a thick roux

Salt and pepper to taste

2 cups klopse stock, skimmed to remove lemon and onion.

Melt butter in medium size pan. Stir in flour. Add stock slowly, and stir constantly. Boil till thickened. Add capers to flavor. Pour over klopse in casserole and serve.

Swiss Steak

12 beef-cube steaks, or 2 steaks per person
1/2 tsp. salt
1/4 tsp. pepper
1/4 cup all-purpose flour
8 oz. can diced tomatoes
3 onions, 1-1 1/2" diced
4 ribs celery, 1-1 1/2" diced
2 carrots, 1-1/2" diced
1/4 tsp. garlic powder
1 bay leaf
Maggi to taste or bouillon cubes
3 tbs. shortening

Salt and pepper steaks and brown them in oil; cover with flour. Put diced vegetables in roasting pan and place browned steaks on top.

Make gravy from steak drippings, added stock and seasonings. Thicken gravy with flour or corn starch, and pour over steak-vegetable mix. Cover pan and bake for 1 hour or until steaks are tender.

Meat Loaf - *Hackbraten*

1 lb. pork
1 1/2 lbs. ground beef
1 med. onion, chopped fine
2 ribs celery, chopped fine
1/3 cup diced tomatoes
1 tbs. sweet relish
3 eggs
1/4 tsp. salt and pepper, or to taste

Mix all ingredients together. Boil 1 carrot tender crisp. Place half the mixture in pan (10 1/2" x 5" x 3"). Put the carrot in the center of mixture and add the remaining mixture. Pour 1/4 cup water over meat, so that foil will not stick to meat. Cover meat with foil and bake at 425° for 1 hour. Remove foil and bake 1/2 hour longer, allowing meat to brown. 6 servings.

Bernie Donahue mixes a drink while Mark Metzger and his dad prepare to wait on a customer.

Pork Tenderloin Tips with Mushroom Sauce

2 lb. pork shoulder meat or small pork roast

3 or 4 med. onions

1 qt. beef stock or water with 2 beef bouillon cubes

4 oz. can mushroom stems and pieces

Salt, pepper, and Maggi to taste

Cut meat into 2" pieces. Put in a roaster and place in pre-heated 425° oven. Allow to brown. Cut onions in 2" pieces. Add onions and stock to browned pork. Stock should cover pork and onions. Cook for about 1 hour or until pork is done. Thicken with a cornstarch roux made with mushroom juice. Add mushrooms, salt and pepper to taste. Color with Kitchen Bouquet, if desired.

Veal Hearts - *Kalbsherz*

2 - 3 lbs. veal hearts

1 med. onion, cut in half

1 cup cider vinegar

1/3 tsp. pickling spice

Put veal hearts in a pot, cover with water and bring to a boil. Let boil for a few minutes. Drain well and cover with fresh water. Add the onion, cider vinegar and pickling spice. Bring to a boil and let boil for one hour.

When hearts are done, remove and discard small veins. Slice into thin, lengthwise slices. Remove onion and pickling spices from stock. Thicken with brown flour, add salt, pepper and Maggi or bouillon cubes. Use Kitchen Bouquet for darker color. Pour gravy over heart slices.

Old German *Goulash*

2 1/2 lbs. stew meat
1 bay leaf
3/4 tsp. paprika
3/4 tsp. garlic powder
1 tsp. salt
1/2 tsp. pepper
2 oz. cider vinegar
2 beef bouillon cubes or Maggi to taste
16 oz. can diced tomatoes
2 qts. stock
6 medium Spanish onions

Cut meat into large pieces and cook until dark brown. This can be done in the oven without stock. When meat is brown, add onions, tomatoes, stock, cider vinegar, paprika, pepper, garlic powder, bay leaf, salt, and bouillon cubes or Maggi. Cook in 425° oven for about 1 1/2 hours. Add cornstarch to thicken gravy.

Sauerbraten

5 - 6 lb. eye of round roast
2 tbs. sugar
1 bay leaf
1 tsp. salt
1/2 tsp. pepper
1/4 cup chili sauce
1 cup apple-cider vinegar
1/2 tbs. garlic powder
1 med. onion, sliced
2/3 cup flour

In large stock pot or Dutch oven, mix all ingredients together, except flour (reserve this for gravy). Add meat. Marinate for 2 - 3 days, turning occasionally. Add enough water to cover 2" above meat. Boil marinated meat for 2 hours over medium-high heat. Keep warm while preparing gravy as follows:

Continue to boil meat marinade juices. Thicken with flour that has been browned in a little margarine. Season with Maggi seasoning and salt. Serve meat with gravy on the side.

Chicken Pie

1 1/2 lbs. cooked chicken

1/2 cup onion, chopped

2/3 cup celery, chopped

Egg shade to color chicken base or bouillon

1 to 2 ozs diced red pepper or pimento, cooked or canned

4 eggs

Cook celery and onion in 2 cups of stock or water until done, and add egg shade to color Add two tbs. flour to cooked celery and onions to thicken. Add diced red pepper. Cut chicken into small pieces and add to chicken base or 1 chicken bouillon cube for added flavor. Add eggs. You may also add ground chicken skin. Mix all filling ingredients well.

Pie crust:

1 1/2 cups flour

2 tbs. shortening

Salt and pepper to taste

Ice water (2-3 oz.)

Blend flour, shortening, salt and pepper together, then add enough ice water to make a stiff dough.

Make a two layer pie crust. Line bottom and sides of a pie dish with first crust, then add chicken filling and place second crust on top. Brush milk on top, and using a fork, make a few holes in top crust. Bake at 425° for 1 hour or until crust is brown.

Stuffed Peppers - *Gefuellte Paprika*

8 green peppers

1 lb. ground pork

1 lb. ground beef

1 cup cooked rice

1/2 cup can deced tomatoes or chopped raw tomatoes

1/2 onion, chopped

2 ribs celery, chopped

Garlic, salt and pepper to taste

Cut tops from peppers and remove seeds. Combine remaining ingredients and use to stuff peppers. Put into casserole dish; pour sauce over peppers and bake covered at 425° for 1 hour or until done. You may remove cover and bake a little longer if the peppers are not brown enough.   Note: Use the same sauce as for stuffed cabbage.

Macaroni and Cheese

1 lb. macaroni

3 cups milk

Egg shade coloring

12 oz. cheddar cheese diced small or you may use any other
        yellow cheese

8 oz. Cheese Whiz

Cook macaroni in salt water until 2/3 done. Drain well. Put macaroni in baking dish. Combine macaroni, diced cheese and Cheese Whiz. Heat milk until it just reaches boiling point, but does not boil. Add egg shade for color and pour over macaroni. Cover and bake at 425° for 1 hour. Let stand for a few minutes to allow sauce to thicken. Top with paprika, if desired.

Side Dishes

Spaetzle

1 2/3 cups flour
3 eggs
1 tsp. salt
5 fl. oz. water (added until right consistency)
For Topping:
1 tbs. butter
1 tbs. dried bread crumbs

Make a smooth, tough dough using spoon or hand-held mixer by adding to flour, eggs, salt and lukewarm water in increments until right consistency is reached. Spread portions of dough on wooden (spaetzle) board and scrape with spaetzle scraper or wide knife. Put slivers of spaetzle dough into rapidly boiling salt water. As soon as spaetzle rises to the surface, remove with spaetzle skimmer and drop into hot water. Immediately place them into a colander to drain. Arrange on heated platter and serve.

Topping:

Heat butter in skillet and add dry bread crumbs; stir till fried golden brown. Spread on top of spaetzle.

Note: Instead of scraping spaetzle, the easier and just as effective way, is to press dough through a special spaetzle maker. Water should be boiling rapidly at all times. Remove spaetzle when they rise to top and when water looks frothy on top.

Apple Pancakes - *Apfelpfannkuchen*

2/3 cup unsifted flour

2 tsp. sugar

1/4 tsp. salt

4 eggs, beaten

1/2 cup milk

2 cups apple slices

3/4 cup butter or margarine

2 tbs. sugar

1/4 tsp. cinnamon

Sift together flour, sugar, and salt. Beat eggs and milk together. Gradually add flour mixture; beat until smooth. Saute apples in 1/4 cup butter until tender. Mix 2 tablespoons sugar and the cinnamon together; toss with apples. Melt 2 tablespoons butter in 6-inch frypan. Pour in batter to a depth of about 1/4 inch. When set, place 1/4 of apples on top; cover with more batter. Fry pancake until lightly browned on both sides. Repeat procedure 3 times, until all batter and apples are used. Serve immediately. Makes 4 pancakes.

Red Cabbage - *Rotkohl*

1 medium head red cabbage
1 apple
2 tbs. brown sugar
2/3 bay leaf
3/4 cup cider vinegar*
2 cups soup stock—beef or chicken
3/4 tsp. salt

Cut cabbage in half then slice. Dice apple and put in pot with remaining ingredients. Cook until done.

*For special flavor you may use a small amount of red wine.

Baked Beans

1 lb. Navy beans
1 cup tomato ketchup
1 cup chili sauce
1/4 cup brown sugar
Ham bone, diced bacon or polish sausage

Cover beans with water and soak over night. Drain water off and cover with fresh water or beef stock. Add ham bone, diced bacon or Polish sausage and cook 1/2 hour or until beans are done, but not overcooked. Put in roaster and add rest of ingredients. Mix well and bake at 425° for about 45 minutes or until done.

Cheese Spatzen Sauerkraut and Fried Onion
- *Kasse Spatzen*

2 tbs. sauerkraut

3 cups spatzen

1 onion - sliced

2 slices Swiss cheese

2 stems green onion

Cook sauerkraut until tender. Fry sliced onion until very dark. In a baking dish, make layers of spatzen, Swiss cheese, green onion and fried onion slices. Add sauerkraut to top of spatzen and bake in oven for 3 to 4 minutes, or micro-wave for 2 minutes. Serve while hot.

Cooked Potato Dumplings
- *Gekochte Kartoffelklösse*

6 medium potatoes, cooked in skins

1/2 to 1 cup flour

2 eggs, beaten

1 tsp. salt

1 cup day-old white bread

Bread crumbs sauteed in 1/2 cup melted butter or margarine

6 to 8 cups hot beef or chicken broth

1/2 cup melted butter

Peel and grate potatoes while warm. Blend in flour, eggs, and salt to form a dough stiff enough to shape with fingers. Shape into balls 2 or 3 inches in diameter. If dumplings do not shape well, add more flour to dough. Force a few fried bread crumbs into the center of each ball; seal over. Reserve rest of crumbs. Cook dumplings in boiling broth until they rise to the top; about 10 minutes, and remove to serving dish. Spoon melted butter over tops; sprinkle with remaining fried bread crumbs. Makes 4 to 6 servings—8 to 12 dumplings, depending on size.

Bread Dumplings - *Brot Knoedel*

24 oz. croutons

4 eggs

1 1/2 medium onions

2 medium cooked potatoes, grated

1 1/2 ribs celery

1/2 tsp. nutmeg

1/4 cup flour

1/4 cup milk

Salt and pepper to taste

Dice celery and onion, add pepper, salt, grated potatoes, nutmeg, eggs and flour. Add milk and croutons; mix well. Let stand 1/2 hour. Bring 2 qts. water and 2 beef bouillon cubes to boil in large pot. Roll dough in flour to form 2 1/2" dumplings. Thicken boiling water with 1 cup of flour/water paste. Add dumplings and simmer 15 minutes.

Creamed Cabbage

1/2 head cabbage (1 - 2 pound size)

1/2 medium onion, finely chopped

1/2 rib celery, finely chopped

1 1/3 cups milk

Salt and pepper to taste

1/4 tsp. caraway seeds

1/4 tsp. savory

Cut cabbage into 3/4" pieces. Cook in water with onion and celery until well done. Drain well and place in serving dish.

Thick white sauce:

4 oz. margarine melted

3/4 cup flour

2 cups milk

Cook until thickened, and pour over cabbage. Mix and serve.

Potato Pancakes - *Kartoffelpfannkuchen*

2 1/2 cups grated raw potatoes

3 cups water

1 tsp. lemon juice

1 boiled or a little mashed potatos if you have it

1 egg, beaten

2 tbs. milk

1/2 tsp. salt

6 to 8 tbs. vegetable oil

Place grated potatoes and lemon juice in water; drain very well. Beat raw and cooked potatoes with egg, milk and salt to form batter. Using 3 tbs. oil for each batch, drop batter for 3 or 4 pancakes into hot oil in large frypan. When firm on bottom side, loosen edges and turn; brown other side. Remove and drain on paper towel.

Potato pancakes are served with meat, or applesauce

Makes 8 to 10 pancakes.

Dave Shepard, Ann Arborites favorite paper boy during the day, worked part time at the Old "G", and stayed on to help in the kitchen.

Creamed Peas

10 oz. fresh or frozen peas
2 tbs. margarine
2 tbs. flour
1 1/2 cups boiling milk

Microwave peas until tender and put in a bowl. Make a white sauce from remaining ingredients. Stir white sauce into peas and top with margarine and serve.

Spinach - *Spinat*

1 pkg. frozen spinach, chopped
1/3 onion
2 slices bacon
1/8 tsp. garlic powder
1/8 tsp. salt and nutmeg to taste

Microwave spinach 3 1/2 minutes. Fry bacon and onion together until lightly brown and tender. Put spinach in a bowl and add fried onion and bacon on top. Pour white sauce over spinach. If you want a more tender spinach, microwave a few more minutes.

Spaetzle Noodles - *Spätzle*

3 cups flour
1 tsp. salt
1/4 tsp. nutmeg
4 eggs, beaten
1/2 cup water (or more)
1/4 cup butter

Sift flour, salt, and nutmeg together in a bowl. Pour eggs and 1/4 cup water into middle of flour mixture; beat with a wooden spoon. Add enough water to make the dough slightly sticky, yet keeping it elastic and stiff. Using a spaetzle machine or a colander with medium holes, press the noodles into a large pot full of boiling salted water. Cook noodles in the water about 5 minutes or until they rise to the surface. Lift noodles out and drain on paper towels. Brown noodles in melted butter over low heat. Makes 4 to 5 servings.

Chicken Dressing

15 - 20 slices bread or rolls
1/2 cup chopped onion
1/2 cup chopped celery
1/4 cup chopped parsley
2 cups chicken or beef stock or bouillon
2 eggs
Nutmeg and sage to taste

Sauté onions and celery in small amount of margarine until transparent. Mix all ingredients together.

Note: To use as a stuffing for pork chops, add one-half pound of ground pork.

Spaetzle Cheese Noodles - *Küsespützle*

3 tbs. butter or margarine
3 onions, sliced in small rings
3 oz. Emmenthaler cheese, grated
1 tsp. dry mustard
2 cups cooked spaetzle noodles or thin noodles
(see recipe for spaetzle on page 48)
2 tbs. chopped chives

Heat butter in a frypan; add onions and brown lightly. Toss cheese with dry mustard. Add cooked noodles to cooked onions and cheese; mix well. Place mixture in an ovenproof casserole. Bake at 300'F for 20 to 30 minutes or until hot and bubbly.

Sprinkle top with chopped chives before serving.

Makes 4 servings.

Sauerkraut

1 onion finely chopped
3 tbs. lard or regular shortening
1 3/4 lbs. of sauerkraut
1 tbs. flour

Saute onion in shortening until light brown. Add sauerkraut and simmer covered 30-40 minutes. Toward end bind sauerkraut with flour blended in a little water. Cook with fresh or smoked pork or bacon to the simmering phase. Serve with the inevitable spaetzle or potatoes.

Note: American sauerkraut is often very salty. We recommend rinsing it in cold water several times before cooking.

Sauces & Gravy

Vanilla Sauce - *Vanill Sosse*

2 cups milk

1/4 cup sugar

1/2 vanilla bean or 1 Tsp.

2 tsp. cornstarch

Vanilla extract

2 egg whites, stiffly beaten

In the top of an enameled double boiler, scald milk with vanilla bean. If you use extract, scald milk, then stir extract in. Beat egg yolks with sugar and cornstarch until light and frothy. Pour vanilla-flavored milk into egg-yolk mixture slowly, stirring vigorously as you do so. Pour mixture back into top of double boiler and set over hot, not boiling, water that does not touch the upper pan. Cook over simmering water, stirring constantly, until sauce becomes custardy and thick enough to coat a wooden spoon. If you would like a foamy sauce, beat egg whites into custard until frothy. Serve hot or cold.

White Sauce - *Weisse Sosse*

2 tbs. margarine

2 tbs. flour

1 1/2 -2 cups boiling milk

Heat margarine and blend in flour. Gradually pour in milk. Stir constantly over low heat until sauce thickens and bubbles.

Brown Sauce - *Braune Sosse*

4 tbs. butter

2 cups cold brown stock

4 tbs. flour

salt to taste

1 small onion, finely minced

Melt butter in 6-cup saucepan; add flour and saute slowly, stirring constantly until it begins to brown. Add finely minced onion, saute a few seconds until onion begins to brown and flour has become a deeper brown. Stir in cold stock all at once, beating with a wire whisk until smooth and well blended. Cover and simmer 30 minutes. Season to taste.

Steak Sauce - *Steak Sosse*

2 onions, chopped

2 tbs. margarine

2 beef bouillon cubes

1 qt. beef stock

1/2 tsp. garlic powder or 1 clove fresh garlic

Sauté onions in margarine until very dark, almost burnt. Add beef stock or water and bouillon cubes. Add seasoning with Maggi. Simmer about 1/2 hour. Strain and add spices to taste.

Mushroom Gravy - *Pilz Sosse*

2 cups mushrooms

1/3 stick margarine

2 onions, thinly sliced

1/3 cup flour

Melt butter, sauté onions until tender then add flour and 2 cups of beef stock or water. Bring to a boil and add mushrooms with juice. Cook, stirring until thickened then pour over meat and serve with noodles.

Tomato Sauce - *Tomaten Sosse*

8 oz. stock or water

1/2 cup chopped celery

1/2 cup chopped onion

1 8 oz. can tomato soup

10 oz. tomato juice

1/3 tsp. garlic powder

Tabasco sauce to taste

1/2 tsp. Maggi or 2 beef bouillon cubes

Bring all ingredients to a boil and thicken with cornstarch.

Mustard - *Senf*

4 oz. dry mustard powder

10 oz. wet mustard/American yellow

Horseradish, to taste

1-2 drops Tabasco sauce and Kitchen Bouquet

8 oz. dark beer (any kind)

Mix all ingredients together well. If mustard is too strong, add sugar to taste. Refrigerate.

Salads

Cole Slaw - *Kraut Salat*

1/2 head cabbage, shredded fine (1 - 1 1/2 lbs.)
1/3 tsp. garlic powder
1/2 tsp. salt
1/2 tsp. pepper
2 oz. pimento, cut fine
1 carrot, shredded fine
3/4 cup mayonnaise
1/3 cup salad oil
2/3 cup cider vinegar
1/2 cup crushed pineapple with juice

Combine all ingredients and let stand for 1/2 hour. Mix together two more times, letting stand for 1/2 hour each time. You may add sweet relish to taste and refrigerate.

Kidney Bean Salad - *Gruene Bohnen Salat*

1 40 oz. can kidney beans
      or, 2 cups dried kidney beans
1/2 onion
1/2 stalk celery
3/4 cup mayonaise
1/2 tsp. sugar
1 tbs. sweet relish

Soak dried beans over night. Cook and rinse with cold water. Rinse canned beans with cold water. Mix all ingredients together and refrigerate.

Nicoise Salata

1 egg
4 oz. can tuna with water
1 cup mayonnaise
Salt and pepper to taste
1/2 cup fresh lemon juice
1 tbs. vinegar
1 tsp. salad oil
1/3 cup milk
1 oz. capers with juice

Blend all ingredients in blender. Pour into a bowl and add capers and juice. Use within 24 hours. Pour over tossed salad. You may use any kind of vegetables, hard boiled eggs, sardines, etc.

Navy Bean Salad

1 lb. navy beans soaked over night
1/2 onion
1/2 rib celery
1 tsp. sugar
1/2 tsp. savory
Salt and pepper to taste
3/4 cup mayonnaise
1 tbs. sweet relish

Cook navy beans until done—do not overcook. Strain and rinse with cold water. Cut celery and onion very fine or use a food chopper. Combine all ingredients together and refrigerate.

Cucumber Salad

2 cucumbers
1 medium onion, sliced fine
2-3 tbs. salad oil
2-3 tbs. cider vinegar
1/4 tsp garlic salt or powder
Salt and pepper
Dash of sugar and dill

Peel cucumbers and slice into transparent, paper-thin slices and mix with salad oil and sliced onion. Let stand for a little while. Shortly before serving, mix in vinegar, salt, pepper, garlic salt and sugar. Sprinkle finely chopped dill over salad mixture.

Green Bean Salad

2 lbs fresh green beans
        or canned green or wax beans
2-3 tbs. salad oil
1 tsp. salt
1 dash pepper
1 finely diced onion
1/2 tsp. dill
1/4 cup cider vinegar

Break the green beans in half and cook in salt water until soft. Cool with cold water and drain. Mix with salt, pepper, finely diced onions, dill, oil and vinegar. Serve

Ochsenmaul Beef Tongue Salad

Dice 1/2 cooked, pealed tongue

      (Recipe for *Ochsenmaul* Beef Tongue on page 27

1 cup cider vinegar

2 large onions

1 tbs. pickling spices

1 tsp. curing salt (Kosher)

1 tsp. sugar

1/2 cup water

1/3 cup cider vinegar

Garlic powder to taste

Place in a quart jar—layering with sliced onions. Mix cider vinegar with water, garlic powder, sugar and pickling spices. Pour over diced tongue and onions to fill jar. Seal and refrigerate. Let stand for several hours before serving. If vinegar taste is too strong, drain and add water. Add a little salad oil before serving.

The ambiance of the Old German Restaurant

Bavarian Sausage Salad
- *Bayerischer Wurstsalat*

1/2 pound knockwurst, cooked and cooled

2 small dill pickles

1 onion

3 tbs. vinegar

1 tsp. strong mustard (Dijon or Gulden)

2 tbs. vegetable oil

1/2 tsp. salt

1/4 tsp. pepper

1/4 tsp. paprika

1/4 tsp. sugar

1 tbs. capers

1 tbs. chopped parsley

Cut knockwurst into small cubes. Mince the pickles and onion. Mix together the vinegar, mustard, and oil. Add salt, pepper, paprika, and sugar. Adjust seasonings, if desired. Add capers and mix well. Stir in the chopped knockwurst, pickles, and onions. Just before serving, garnish with chopped parsley. Makes 4 servings.

Potato Salad - *Kartoffel Salat*

8 medium potatoes

1/4 cup finely sliced white onion

1/4 cup salad oil

1/4 cup plus 2 tbs. cider vinegar

1 finely sliced green onion

3/4 - 1 cup warm beef or chicken broth

Salt and pepper to taste

Cook potatoes (but do not overcook), peel hot and let stand. After potatoes are cooled, slice medium thin. Mix in remaining ingredients. Let stand for 1/2 hour. Serve at room temperature. Refrigerate any left over.

Deserts

There was little baking done at The Old German Restaurant. Mainly bread pudding and rice pudding were prepared daily. Most breads and deserts were supplied by German bakeries, including cakes and pastries for special occasions.

Prince Regent Luitpold's Cake
- *Prinzregententort*

This "Torte" was created for Prince Regent Luitpold. It's eight layers symbolizing the eight governmental districts, i.e.: Upper Bavaria, Lower Bavaria, Upper Palatinate, Upper Franconia, Central Franconia, Lower Franconia, Swabia, and the left-bank Rhine Palatinate, which belonged to Bavaria in the years 1815-1946. It remains open to debate, however, which Bavarian district lies on the chocolate side. . . .

1/2 lb. sweet butter
2 whole eggs
2 egg yolks
1/2 lb. sugar
1/2 lb. flour
1 tbs. vanilla
2 tbs. dark rum
1 pinch salt
2 egg whites beaten with 1/2 tsp. lemon juice

Stir butter vigorously until foamy. Gradually add sugar, salt, egg yolks, whole eggs, rum, and vanilla and beat till creamy. Add flour and stiffly beaten egg whites to make a smooth dough. Spread the bottom of a well-buttered 8" springform pan with approximately 2 tbs. of mixture, making it thicker around the edges. Bake 8 layers 6-8 minutes this way in preheated 350° oven. Cool layers on greaseproof paper in a stack and weigh with a heavy object to keep them flat.

Continued on next page

Prince Regent Luitpold's Cake
Filling:

7 oz. semi-sweet chocolate

7 oz. butter

3 egg yolks

4 oz. sugar

5 oz. sweet chocolate

Melt chocolate, beat butter and sugar and stir into chocolate; add egg yolks and beat until foamy. Spread mixture on the baked layers alternately, but leave top layer free. Spread top layer with thin layer of apricot jam, than coat with a chocolate glaze. Let cake stand for one day before serving.

Bread Pudding - *Brot Pudding*

8 slices toasted white bread

1 apple or apple sauce

3- 4 eggs

3 tbs. sugar

1/4 tsp. vanilla

4 tbs. raisins

1 qt. milk.

Place toast in layers in a 9" x 12" pan. Sprinkle with raisins and finely sliced apples. Sprinkle each layer with cinnamon until all toast is used. In a separate bowl, beat eggs and add vanilla and sugar. Pour boiling milk over eggs and stir. Pour mixture over bread, cover and bake at 425° for 30-40 minutes. Serve with vanilla sauce.

Rice Pudding - *Reis Pudding*

2 cups cooked rice, not overcooked
4 tbs. raisins
4 large eggs
1 tsp. vanilla
5 tbs. sugar
4 1/2 cups milk
Cinnamon

Place cooked rice in a 8" baking dish and sprinkle with raisins. Beat eggs. Heat milk almost to a boil; stir in sugar and vanilla and add to eggs. Pour over rice and bake at 425° until golden brown and custard is set. Sprinkle with cinnamon.

Cinnamon Stars - *Zimtsterne*

6 egg whites
1 lb. powdered sugar
1 lb. ground almonds
2 tsp. cinnamon
Pinch salt

Mix egg whites and powdered sugar. Reserve 6 tsp for topping. Mix all ingredients and refrigerate over night. Roll out onto a floured board, 1/4" thick, and cut with star cutter. Place stars on greased and floured cookie sheet, Spread with reserved egg and sugar mixture. Bake at 325° for 12 minutes.

Sugar Cookies

1 stick butter - softened

2 cups sugar

3 eggs - well beaten

2 tbs. milk

5 cups flour

1 tsp. salt

1 1/2 tsp. baking soda

1 1/2 tsp. cream of tartar

3 tsp. vanilla

Sift flour, baking soda, salt and cream of tartar together and mix. Cream butter and add sugar; add eggs and vanilla. Add dry ingredient, alternating with milk.

Roll 1/8" thick and cut with cookie cutter. Bake in preheated 350 ° oven for 12 to 15 minutes. Cool cookies on racks. Store in airtight tins.

Bud Metzger and his sister, Bertha Metzger Wittke

Cheesecake - *Kaesekuchen*

Crust:

2 cups flour - sifted

1/2 cup sugar

1/2 stick butter

1 egg - large

1 to 2 tbs. brandy, cognac or rum

Sift flour into a bowl and add remaining ingredients. Kneed with fingers to make a smooth paste and form into a ball. Chill for 1 hour and roll to fit a 9" spring form pan. Chill again and bake for 15 minutes.

Filling:

1 1/2 lbs. cream cheese

6 large eggs- separated

1 1/3 cups sugar

2 tbs. flour

1 3/4 cups sour cream

2 tsp. grated lemon rind

2 tsp. lemon juice

1 1/2 tsp. vanilla extract

Combine cheese and egg yolks and beat with electric beater until well blended and smooth. Continue to beat and gradually add 1 cup of sugar, flour, sour cream and flavorings. Beat until light and smooth. Beat egg whites to form soft peaks and fold in remaining 1/3 cup sugar and cheese mixture; pour into crust. Bake at 325° for 70 to 75 minutes. Turn off oven and let cake cool in oven with door open.

Spritz Cookies - *Spritzgebäck*

1 cup butter

2/3 cup confectioner's sugar

1 egg

1 egg yolk

1 tsp. almond or lemon extract

2 1/4 cups unsifted flour

1/4 tsp. salt

1/2 tsp. baking powder

Cream butter and sugar until light. Beat in egg, egg yolk and extract. Sift flour, salt, and baking powder. Gradually add flour mixture to eggs. Chill dough 1/2 hour.

Press 1/4 of dough into cookie press. Keep remaining dough chilled. Shape cookies onto greased baking sheet. Bake in 400° oven for 7 to 10 minutes, until done. Cool on wire racks. Store in airtight tins.

Spice Cookies - Gewürzplätzchen

1/2 cup butter or margarine

1/4 cup shortening

1 cup brown sugar, firmly packed

1 egg

1/4 cup molasses

2 1/2 cups unsifted flour

1/4 tsp. salt

2 tsp. baking soda

1 tsp. cinnamon

1/2 tsp. ginger

1/2 tsp. ground cloves

1/2 tsp. ground allspice

Cream butter, shortening and brown sugar thoroughly. Blend in egg and molasses. Sift together remaining ingredients and sift into sugar mixture. Shape dough into 3/4" balls. Place 2" apart on greased baking sheet. Flatten each ball with the bottom of a glass that has been greased and dipped in sugar. Bake in preheated 350° oven for 12 to 15 minutes. Cool on racks and store in airtight tins.

Springerle

4 eggs

1 pound sugar

1 pound of flour

1 teaspoon baking powder

1/4 teaspoon cream of tartar.

Butter the size of a walnut

1 tear (drop) lemon juice.

Beat eggs for 15 minutes; gradually add sugar and beat another 15 minutes. Sift together flour, baking powder and cream of tartar. Add butter, and lemon juice. Grease pan with butter. Add flour mixture to egg and sugar mixture. Let stand in bowl 2 to 3 hours in refrigerator. With a floured rolling pin, roll out dough to 3/8 inch thickness. Flour a springerle board and press or roll design on dough. Let stand over night in cool place. Bake at 300° in preheated oven for about 10 minutes.

Pepper Balls - *Pfeffernüsse*

6 cups unsifted flour

1 tsp. baking powder

1 tsp. cinnamon

1 tsp. cloves

1/2 tsp. mace

1 tsp. ground allspice

Dash to 1/4 tsp. black pepper

1 1/4 cups honey

2 tbs. butter

2 eggs

1 cup confectioner's sugar

1 tsp. vanilla

1 to 2 tbs. water

Sift flour, baking powder and spices. Heat honey and butter until melted. Cool to luke warm and beat in egg. Add flour mixture. Chill dough 1/2 hour.

Shape dough into 1" balls. Place on greased cookie sheet and bake at 350° for 15 minutes. Cool cookies on wire rack.

Mix confectioner's sugar, vanilla and water to form a thin glaze. Dip cookies in glaze and place on wire rack to dry. Store cookies in airtight container. Makes 4 dozen cookies.

Almond Crescents -*Mandel-halbmonde*

1 cup butter or margarine
3/4 cup sugar
1 tsp. vanilla extract
1 1/2 tsp. almond extract
2 1/2 cups flour
1 cup ground almonds
Confectioner's sugar

Beat butter and sugar together until light and fluffy. Blend in extracts Mix in flour and almonds.

Use 1 tbs. of dough for each crescent; shape into logs and bend into crescents. Bake 12 to 14 minutes at 350° until light brown. While warm, roll in confectioner's sugar. Cool on racks and store in airtight container.

Marzella Leib
a favorite
Old German
waitress for 30
years.

Sand Tarts - *Sandörtchen*

2 1/2 cups sugar
2 cups butter or margarine
2 eggs
4 cups unsifted flour
1 egg white, beaten
Sugar
Cinnamon
Pecan halves

Cream sugar and butter and beat in whole eggs. Gradually blend in flour. Chill dough overnight. Roll as thin as possible on well-floured board. Work with 1/4 of dough at a time. Keep remaining dough chilled. Cut into diamonds and place on greased cook sheet. Brush each cookie with beaten egg white; sprinkle with sugar and pinch of cinnamon. Place a pecan in center of each cookie. Bake in preheated 350° oven 8 to 10 minutes, until edges are slightly browned. Cool on cookie sheets for 1 minute; remove to wire racks. Store in airtight tins. Makes 9 dozen cookies.

Spice Bars - *Lebkuchen*

1 tsp. cinnamon

1 tsp ground allspice

1/4 tsp. ground cloves

1/2 tsp. salt

2 1/4 cups unsifted flour

1/2 tsp. baking powder

1/2 cup ground almonds

1 tsp. grated lemon rind

2 eggs

3/4 cup sugar

3/4 cup honey

1/2 cup milk

Sift together spices, salt, flour and baking powder. Stir in almonds and lemon rind. In separate bowl, beat eggs and sugar until a ribbon is formed when beater if removed. Stir in honey and milk. Gradually stir in flour mixture and beat until smooth. Spread batter in a well greased and floured 11" x 17" jelly-roll pan. Bake in 400° oven for 12 to 15 minutes until done. While still warm, turn cake onto a rack.

Almond Glaze

1 cup confectioner's sugar

1/2 tsp. almond extract

1 tsp. rum

1 to 2 tbs. water

Mix all ingredients and beat until smooth. Spread over warm cake. Cut into 1" x 2 1/2" bars. Keep in sealed container.

Apple Cake - *Blitzkuchen Mit Apfeln*

10 oz. flour

1/4 lb. butter

1/4 lb. butter

2 eggs

1 tbs. rum

2 lbs. tart apples

1 oz. butter

4 tbs. raisins soaked in rum

2 tbs. chopped candied orange peel

1 egg yolk

2 tbs. almonds

Sift flour onto pastry board; add butter in flakes and sprinkle with sugar. Add eggs and rum. Mix and knead quickly into a dough, cover and let rest for 1/2 hour. Peel and thinly slice apples and saute 3 to 4 minutes in butter and let cool. Roll out 1/2 dough into a circle large enough to cover bottom and sides of 10" buttered springform pan. Mix apple slices, raisins and orange peel and pour into lined form. Roll out remaining dough to cover top of cake; press down to seal. Punch holes into top layer to allow steam to escape. Brush top with egg yolk and garnish with almond halves, pressing down firmly to hold. Bake in preheated 420° oven for 40 to 45 minutes.

Topping

3 1/2 oz. confectioner's sugar

1 tbs. Arrack

1 tbs. hot water.

Mix sifted sugar with liquids and pour over hot cake. Let cool before removing spring form. Serve with a bowl of whipped cream.

Apple and Rum Custard Cake - *Rahmapfelkuehen*

Crust

1 1/2 cups unsifted flour

5 tbs. sugar

1 tbs. grated lemon rind

2/3 cup butter or margarine

1 egg yolk

1 tbs. milk

Mix flour, sugar and lemon rind. Cut in butter until mixture resembles coarse crumbs. Add egg yolk and 1 tbs. milk; mix gently to form dough. Grease sides of 10" springform pan; pat dough into bottom of pan and press up 1" of sides.

Filling

1/2 cup soft bread crumbs

2 tbs. melted butter or margarine

4 cups of sliced tart apples

1 tbs. lemon juice

1/4 cup sugar

1/4 cup raisins, soaked 1/2 hour in 1/4 cup rum

Toss together bread crumbs and melted butter, and spread evenly over crust. Toss apple slices, lemon juice, and 1/4 cup sugar. Spread apples over crumbs. Drain raisins, reserving rum, and sprinkle raisins over apples.

Custard

3 eggs beaten

1/3 cup sugar

1 3/4 cups milk

Beat eggs and sugar until thick and lemon colored. Stir in milk and reserved rum. Pour custard over apples and bake for 45 to 60 minutes at 350° until custard is set. Remove springform pan when completely cool and serve.

Black Forest Cherry Cake
Schwarzwälder Kirschtorte

6 eggs

1 cup sugar

1 tsp. vanilla

4 sqs. unsweetened baking chocolate, melted

1 cup sifted flour

Beat eggs, sugar and vanilla together until thick and fluffy. Alternately fold chocolate and flour into egg mixture, ending with flour. Pour batter into 3 8" round cake pans that have been well greased and floured. Bake in preheated 350° oven for 10 to 15 minutes. Cool in pans for 5 minutes; turn out on racks to cool completely.

Syrup

1/4 cup sugar

1/3 cup water

2 tbs. Kirsch liquor

Boil sugar and water for 5 minutes; cool. Stir Kirsch into cooled syrup. Prick cake layers and pour syrup over all three layers.

Filling

1 1/2 cups confectioner's sugar

1/3 cup unsalted butter

1 egg yolk

2 tbs. Kirsch liquor

Beat together butter and sugar until well blended. Add egg yolk and beat until light and fluffy. Fold in Kirsch liquor.

(Continued on next page)

Black Forest Cherry Cake
Schwarzwälder Kirschtorte

continued

Topping

2 cups drained, canned sour cherries - pat dry

2 tbs. confectioner's sugar

1 cup heavy cream, whipped

8 oz. semisweet chocolate bar - room temperature

Assemble cake

Place one layer on cake plate and spread with cream filling; drop 3/4 cup cherries evenly over filling. Add second layer and repeat. Add third layer on top. Fold confectioners's sugar into whipped cream and use to decorate top and sides of cake. Decorate top with remaining cherries.

Chocolate Curls

Shave semisweet chocolate bar with vegetable peeler. Refrigerate curls until ready to use. Press curls on sides of cake and sprinkle a few on top. Keep chilled until serving time. Makes 8 to 10 servings.

Apple Strudel - *Apel Strudel*

Makes 2 Strudels:
6 cups sliced tart apples
3/4 cup raisins
1 tbs. grated lemon rind
3/4 cup sugar
2 tsp. cinnamon
3/4 cup ground almonds
1/2 box (16 oz.) frozen fillo leaves, thawed
1 3/4 cups butter or margarine, melted
1 cup fine bread crumbs

Mix apples, raisins, lemon rind, sugar, cinnamon, and almonds. Set aside. Place 1 fillo leaf on a kitchen towel and brush with melted butter. Repeat until 5 leaves have been used, using 1/2 cup butter.

Cook and stir the bread crumbs with 1/4 cup butter until lightly browned. Sprinkle 3/8 cup crumbs on the layered fillo leaves. Mound 1/2 of the filling in a 3" strip along the narrow edge of the fillo, leaving a 2" border. Lift towel, using it to roll leaves over apples, jelly-roll fashion. Brush strudel with butter after each turn. Using towel, place strudel on greased baking sheet. Brush top with butter and sprinkle with 2 tbs. crumbs. Repeat the entire procedure for the second strudel. Bake strudels at 400° for 20 to 25 minutes, until brown. Serve warm.

Swabian Pancakes - *Flädle überbacken*

1 1/4 cups flour

3 eggs

1/2 tsp. salt

2 cups milk

1 tsp. vegetable oil

1 16 oz. can applesauce

4 oz. raisins

2 tbs. sugar

3 tbs. sliced blanched almonds

1 tbs. butter

Blend flour, 2 eggs, 1/4 tsp. salt, and 1 cup milk. Lightly oil frypan and cook 6 to 8 pancakes. Heat applesauce and stir in raisins. Divide sauce between pancakes and spread over top of each. Roll each pancake like a small jelly roll and cut in half with a sharp knife.

Place pancakes in a greased ovenproof dish; setting them up on the cut edge. Blend remaining egg with sugar, salt, milk and sliced almonds. Pour over pancakes. Dot with butter. Bake in preheated 375° oven for 40 minutes. Serve immediately.

Breads

Gugelhupf

1 pkg. active dry yeast

1 cup milk, scalded and cooled

1 cup sugar

1 cup butter or margarine

5 eggs

1 tsp. vanilla

Rind of one lemon, grated

3/4 cup raisins

1/3 cup ground almonds (2 oz. pkg.)

4 cups unsifted flour

Sprinkle yeast in milk to dissolve. In large bowl, beat sugar and butter until light and fluffy. Beat in eggs, one at a time. Stir in vanilla, lemon rind, raisins and almonds. Mix salt and flour. Alternately add milk and flour mixture, ending with flour. Pour batter into a greased gugelhopf mold.* Cover and let rise until double in bulk, about 2 hours. Bake in preheated 375° oven until brown and done. Serve warm with butter.

*This bread is traditionally baked in a *gugelhopf* pan or turban-head pan. If these are unavailable, a bundt pan or tube pan may be used.

Christmas Fruit Bread - *Hutzelbrot*

1 lb. dried prunes

1 lb. dried pears

1 lb. dried figs

2 lbs. pitted dates

Powdered cloves

1/2 lb. shelled walnuts

1/2 lb shelled almonds - unblanched

1/4 lb. candied citron

1/4 lb. candied orange peel

2 tsp. dried yeast

1/2 cup warm water

1 cup lukewarm water in which fruit cooked

10 cups sifted flour

1/4 cup sugar

1 tsp. cinnamon

1 tbs. crushed anise seeds

1 tsp. salt

Almonds - split or slivered

Soak prunes and pears, remove stones, and cook until slightly tender; drain and save liquid. Chop into large pieces. Chop figs, citron and orange peel, walnuts, and almonds finely. Combine all fruits and nuts. Mix yeast in cup of flour and dissolve in warm liquid saved from fruit; add flour, spices and salt. Gradually work in remaining flour and beat until dough blisters and comes away from sides of bowl. Shape dough into ball; set in warm place to rise until double in bulk. Mix risen dough with fruit and nuts; let dough rise again for 45 minutes to an hour. Divide dough in half and form round or oblong loaves. Place on buttered, floured baking sheet. Decorate tops with almonds and citron. Bake 1 hour in 400° oven. Brush with fruit liquid while hot.

Yeast Dough - *Hefeteig*

In every part of Bavaria yeast dough constitutes the basis for a large variety of breads, pastries and cakes. Since yeast is a biological leavener, its use should take preference over the use of chemical leaveners. There is no need to be apprehensive about handling it:if you follow the procedure outlined below, your yeast dough should always be a success:

1. All ingredients should have the same temperature.
2. Salt and fat should never come into direct contact with the yeast.
3. The dough should never be exposed to a draft when it is rising.
4. Prepare a preliminary dough to test the yeast and shorten the rising time.

> 1 3/4 lbs. flour
> 2 oz. yeast
> 1 tbs. sugar
> 3 tbs. lukewarm milk
> 1/4 lb. butter - or margarine
> 1 tbs. lard - or clarified butter
> 1/4 lb. sugar
> 1 tbs. vanilla sugar
> Pinch of salt
> 1/2 - 1 cup lukewarm milk
> 2 eggs

Sift flour into a large, pre-warmed bowl and put in a warm place. Crumble yeast into a cup and mix with the sugar and milk. Make a small depression in the center of the flour; pour in the yeast mixture and mix in handful of flour. Add butter and lard or clarified butter cut into small flakes and distribute over the flour "ring". Sprinkle the sugar,vanilla sugar, and salt over it. Cover with a clean cloth and let rest for approximately 10 minutes. Using a large-headed cooking spoon,beat mixture first with the flour and then with the lukewarm milk until bubbles form in the dough. Cover again and let rise for approx. 3/4 - 1 hour or until the dough has doubled in volume. Use this dough for pleated yeast and, yeast dumplings, etc.

Sourdough Starter - *Sauerteig Starter*

2 cups like warm water or milk
2 cups unbleached, all-purpose flour
2 1/2 tsp. yeast

Mix ingredients together in a glass or plastic bowl. Cover bowl with a tight fitting lid and allow to sit in a warm place for 4 to 7 days. Gently stir once a day.

Sourdough may be used after 4 days.

Mixed Rye Bread - *Roggenmischbrot*

4 cups rye flour
4 cups all purpose flour
2 tsp. dry yeast
5 tsp. salt
1 cup sourdough
1 1/2 cups water

Mix dry yeast into flour, combine flour, sourdough and water; add salt and knead until very smooth—at least 8 minutes. Let sit for about 1-1/2 hours or until dough has doubled. Shape into three oblong loaves and place on lightly floured kitchen towel. Cover and let sit for about one hour. Place on lightly greased cookie sheet, brush with water; make diagonal slashes with a single-edged, razor blade. Bake in 450° preheated oven for 20 minutes. Reduce heat to 325° and bake for another 30 minutes. When taking out of the oven brush again lightly with water and put on a cooling rack.

Old German Muffins - *Aldeutsche Brötchen*

3/4 cup butter or margarine

1/2 cup sugar

2 eggs

1 tbs. rum

1 tsp. vanilla

3 tbs. milk

1/2 tsp. cinnamon

2 tsp. baking powder

2 1/4 cups flour

1/4 cup ground almonds

1 tbs. grated orange rind

1/4 cup raisins

Cream butter and sugar; beat in eggs, rum, vanilla and milk. Mix cinnamon, baking powder, and flour. Add flour mixture to butter mixture. Gently mix in almonds, orange rind, and raisins. Pour batter into greased muffin tins, filling half full. Bake in preheated oven at 375° for 25 to 30 minutes until brown.

Makes 18 muffins.

Reflections

By Grace Shackman

The history of the Old German restaurant is a history of downtown Ann Arbor, which eventually is a history of everything happening worldwide in the summer of 1928.

Patrons of the Old German Restaurant often had to stand in long lines, but the food was worth the wait and they came again and again. The food was justly popular with the city's German population who enjoyed eating their native cuisine. (At one time about half of Ann Arbor's population was of German origin, mainly from Swabia in southern Germany.) But people with no ties to Germany also appreciated the food, just because it tasted so good.

Visitors from Germany always commented on the authenticity of the food. Owner Bud Metzger and chief cook Bill Dettling, both of southern German descent, used recipes handed down from their mothers as well as recipes from the restaurant's former cooks. They added dishes tasted on trips abroad or from other German restaurants they visited. Using fresh ingredients and cooking everything from scratch, they created their own versions of Swabian mainstays. A meat and potatoes cuisine, cooked in an earlier age for people who did physical labor all day, the menu included many special cuts of meat-pork hocks, short ribs in a brown crust, cured shanks, tongue cured in pickling brine, sauerbraten made with a special cut of eye of round and served with a sauce different from the other German restaurants in town, and koenigburger klops (veal meatballs in a caper sauce). German meat patties, a big favorite, were so dubbed after the health department said they could not be called hamburgers because they added other ingredients, although that is what gave them such a good taste.

The side dishes were also unique. Potato Salad served hot was a house specialty. Spatzen, a noodle that originated in Swabia, was made from a dough pushed through a press. Variations included liver spatzen soup. Rolls mops were herring and pickle fried and marinated. Homemade applesauce was a specialty as were apple pancakes.

The restaurant was named the *Old German* by William Schwartz, a German-trained butcher with a specialty in sausage making. In 1928, with the help of his wife Anny, he opened a small lunchroom at 117 S. Ashley in what had been a tire shop. Originally just a counter with a few tables, they expanded around the comer into space formerly held by a grocery store until they eventually faced Washington and just used the Ashley Street door as a back entrance.

When prohibition ended in 1933, Schwarz, still a German citizen, was unable to get a liquor license. He sold the restaurant but took it back a few years later and asked Gottlob Schumacher, a tailor who had boarded at his house when he first came to this country, to be his partner, since he had already obtained citizenship. By then Anny Schwarz had found other employment, but Gottlob's wife Caroline, who learned to cook when in the employ of Dean Meyers, a prominent eye doctor, was able to take over. They prepared daily specials including corned beef and cabbage, chicken potpie ("it went over like crazy," recalls Schumacher), and pig hocks and sauerkraut. Friday was fish day and Sunday was chicken.

The customers, recalls Schumacher, were "lots of Germans from the Second and Third Wards [the west side of town]." Workers from nearby factories, such as King Seeley, American Broach, and International Radio (later Argus), where lots of German craftsmen were employed, arrived in two shifts for lunch. German bachelors bought meal tickets so they could eat their dinners there. "Lots of Americans also liked spatzen, liver dumplings, sauerbraten, broad noodles for goulash, stuffed noodles. If they were prepared right, they went over," recalls Schumacher.

But it was a hard life. Schwarz opened in the morning, cutting the meat needed for the day's menu and working with the morning chef to serve breakfast, starting at 5 am. Schumacher came in at noon and stayed until late at night. The rest of staff worked staggered hours during the day. After Schwarz died of a heart attack, Schumacher ran the restaurant by himself for a few years, but tiring of the long hours, sold it in 1946 to Fritz and Bertha Metzger, who had been running the German Inn on Huron Street.

Fritz Metzger had trained as a baker in Germany before leaving in 1926 to escape rampant inflation. His father had owned a bakery in Germany. Fritz and his two brothers continued in the tradition with Gottfried running a bakery here (the DeLuxe), and William a restaurant that became Metgzers. When Fritz's son Bud (Robert) returned from World War 11, he took an active roll in his parents' establishment, taking over in 1952. Bill Dettling, who had worked as a dishwasher before leaving for the war, also returned to the restaurant. Not wanting to spend the rest of his life in soapy water, Dettling began learning other aspects of restaurant work-waiting tables (although it was then considered more of a woman's job), and helping in the kitchen. Eventually Fritz Metzger decided to teach him cooking.

During the time of post-war prosperity and before the big restaurant boom, the Old German became a premier place to eat in Ann Arbor. Still catering to the town's large German population, the restaurant also served non-German townspeople and university students and professors. It became a place to go to celebrate important anniversaries, passing difficult exams, and entertaining relatives and friends from out of town. Generations of college alumni ate at the Old German on return visits to town. Bud was always around greeting customers and making them feel welcome, while Bill in the kitchen insured that the food maintained its good quality year after year.

The restaurant closed in 1995. Although Bud's customers understood that after almost 50 years of working seven days a week he deserved a rest, they still miss his food. Marzella Leib, a waitress at the restaurant, has worked to preserve the memory of the food. Working with Dettling to put down on paper what he did and in small enough portions so it can be made at home, they created the recipes in this book. Now thanks to their work, people can again enjoy the wonderful food that they used to eat at the Old German.

About the Author
Marzella Leib

It was a long journey that brought me to the doors of the Old German Restaurant. I grew up in a small village in West Germany, not far from Stuttgart. My father was a bricklayer and my mother a midwife. I was one of six children. Times were tough and money and opportunities were far and few between. My dream as a little girt was to use my God given talent to become a famous singer, but that was out of the question. I was performing in a local play when I caught the eye of a fellow villager who was home on vacation from his new life in Canada. We wrote letters to each other for two years, and in 1958 he came to Germany to marry me. Three days later, I left my family behind and accompanied my new husband, Franz, to Canada. Our goal was always to settle in the United States, but we did not have the required sponsor to allow us into the country. Then in 1961 the Quality Bakery, another long time Ann Arbor establishment, agreed to sponsor us.

Shortly after arriving in Ann Arbor, I applied for a job as a waitress at the Old German and Bud Metzger hired me on the spot. The restaurant grew on me and became such a part of my life that I continued working there for over 30 years. Every time I told myself that I had worked there long enough, I just could not bring myself to leave. It was my enjoyment of working for the Metzger family, the authentic German cuisine, the German atmosphere, and most of all the customers that kept me there so long.

I wrote this book to memorialize the recipes of the German food that was loved by so many. I thought it would have been a shame to not leave some sort of history behind from this famous local establishment— The Old German Restaurant.

NOTES

NOTES

NOTES

NOTES

NOTES

NOTES